Fun Methods to avoid prostate cancer

A SUMMARY GUIDE TO SELF-DEVELOPMENT FROM CANCER IN MEN

Dr. Reginna Nile

Dr. Reginna Nile

INTRODUCTION

CONTEXT ONE

RISK FACTORS
DIAGNOSIS

CONTEXT TWO

FUN WAYS TO AVOID PROSTATE CANCER
EXERCISING SHOULD BE A HABIT
Different advantages include:
What practice precautionary measures would it be a good idea for me to take?
Basic precautionary measures to take
Additionally, assuming you experience any of the secondary effects beneath, quit practicing and illuminate your PCP
DIET CONTROL IS PARAMOUNT
FOOD VARIETIES TO EAT AND KEEP AWAY FROM
SELF-MEDICATION
SMOKING
DRINKING OF COFFEE
HEALTHY WEIGHT
The Connection Between Prostate Disease and Your Weight
Why Weight Matters

It Is Great for You to Shed pounds
MASTURBATING
Bringing down prostate cancer risk
21 times each month

CONCLUSION

Dr. Reginna Nile

INTRODUCTION

Prostate disease is quite possibly of the most well-known malignant growth in males. Anyway, paces of the location of prostate tumors change broadly across the world, with Europe and the United States identifying higher recurrence than South and East Asia. In China, the occurrence rate is 1.6 cases per 100000, while 119.9 cases per 100000 in the USA. Prostate cancer will in general foster after the age of fifty in men, however, unfortunately, numerous patients don't have side effects, they try not to take treatment, and in the end, bite the dust. The reasons behind this might be the sluggish developing instances of prostate cancer, and more established individuals might pass on from different causes like heart/circulatory sickness, pneumonia, other unconnected tumors, or advanced age. Albeit two-thirds of cases of prostate diseases are slow developing, there are some instances of forceful prostate diseases. Late confirmations from the Prostate, Lung, Colorectal, and Ovarian Cancer Screening Trial (PLCO), and the European Randomized Investigation of Screening for Prostate Cancer recommended a high pace of overdiagnosis, and overtreatment of prostate cancer, which causes a low death rate compared with the incidence rate throughout recent many years (2, 3). Despite these aftereffects of the previous preliminaries and the achievement, the high mediation pace of prostate disease proceeds. Unfortunately, the anticipation might affect sickness-related mortality. Principally, medical procedures, radiation treatment, and proton pillar treatment are the ongoing treatment choices for prostate cancer growth. Nonetheless, chemotherapy, hormonal treatment, cryosurgery, and focused energy-centered ultrasound (HIFU) are additionally having a place with the treatment strategies, contingent upon clinical circumstances, and results.

Additionally, the decision of treatment relies upon the phases of the sickness movement, the degree of prostate explicit antigen (PSA), and the Gleason score among others. Patients' age, general medical issues, the advantage of therapies, and what's more, their conceivable secondary effects may likewise impact picking among various treatment choices. Any of the treatments might make a huge side-impacts, so the treatment conversations frequently center around adjusting the objectives of treatment with the dangers of the way of life changes. Dietary administration and other life alterations for patients with prostate disease have additionally shown a few positive outcomes to control and forestall prostate cancer. Patients with prostate cancer are firmly prescribed to intently work with their doctors, and utilize a blend of the treatment choices while dealing with their prostate disease (4, 5). The ideal administration of prostate cancer growth remains disputable. This survey article sums up the current treatment and avoidance techniques with the security of prostate disease, which might be useful to control and forestall this exceptionally incessant dangerous sickness. It's assessed that 1 out of 8 American men will be determined to have prostate cancer growth every year. The chances are considerably higher for Black men as they're bound to not exclusively be determined to have the sickness yet, in addition, to pass on from it. While there are sure gamble factors for prostate disease that are beyond your reach, there are not many that you can without much of a stretch location. By handling these regions, you can essentially lessen your probability of fostering the illness.

Prostate disease is one of the most well-known sorts of malignant growth. Numerous prostate tumors develop gradually and are restricted to the prostate organ, where they may not hurt. Be that as it may, while certain kinds of the prostate disease develop gradually and may require negligible or even no treatment, different sorts are forceful and can spread rapidly.

A prostate disease that is identified early when it's bound to the prostate organ has the most obvious opportunity for fruitful treatment.

Prostate cancer growth is the most well-known disease and the main source of malignant growth demise in men more than 50 y in Mexico. In 2015, 41 210 malignant growth passings are normal among men, 6 801 of which will be from PC. Prostate-explicit antigen (PSA) has been applied as a helpful marker for the early conclusion and checking of PC. A randomized concentrate in Europe showed a dynamic decline in prostate cancer growth mortality, with a 51% decrease in people as long as 75 years of age who went through screening. As there is no threatening growth follow-up library in Mexico, PC pervasiveness and the subsequent effect of public service announcement screening can't be precisely estimated. Various key prognostic elements for PC (among others 3,4) have been thought of: Public service announcement assurance: men under 40 years with PSA > 1 ng/mL present a higher PC risk furthermore, ought to be intermittently checked. Illness stage at analysis: 70-80% of cases are limited to the prostate. The Gleason evaluating framework (PC separation grade evaluated by prostate biopsy): 75-80% of cancers are reasonably separated.

CONTEXT ONE
RISK FACTORS

Prostate cancer (PC), age, and heredity, especially grandparents, guardians, kin, or other direct relations with a background marked by the bosom, ovarian or cervical growths, are the main two gamble factors connected with PC advancement.

1. Age. Some 36.3% of cases are analyzed during the seventh 10 years, with 31.6% somewhere in the range of 70 and 79 years.

2. Heredity. PC may be genetic in 10% of cases, with around 2-to 3-crease expanded risk, which increments to up to 5-overlay greater risk assuming that more than one relative is impacted. Besides, a few qualities have been perceived to be engaged with PC improvement, which makes it a polygenic illness. Studies have uncovered the utility of estimating polymorphisms in qualities like ELAC2 (with a job in tubulin capability), RNASEL (an endoribonuclease that goes about as a growth silencer quality), and MSR1 (transformations in this quality present an inclination to persistent fiery conditions) to foresee growth conduct and aggressiveness.

3. Race. In the United States of America (USA), there are 250 000 new PC cases and 27 000 passings each year. More than half of these passings happen among African Americans, trailed by whites, Hispanic-Americans also, less normally among Asians. The chance of creating a PC is 17%, and demise from a similar reason is 3%.

4. Aggravation. Irritation has been proposed as a gamble factor for PC, especially ongoing inflammatory processes influencing the prostate. In any case, this is a dubious contention, and no causality has been affirmed.

5. Chemicals. The interest in androgens also, estrogens at the beginning of PC is notable. Patients with innate androgen inadequacies seldom create PC or prostatic hyperplasia (PH). In any case, if androgen removal is performed after adolescence, these patients may foster PC or PH.

6. Metabolic disorder. The presence of at least two parts of metabolic disorder has been related to a higher gamble of PC, repeat, or potentially progression.

7. There are various investigations on the defensive jobs of nutrients E and D, selenium, calcium, and omega 3 and 6 unsaturated fats in the counteraction of PC. Be that as it may, no authoritative reason impact relationship has been found. People who consume a Mediterranean diet high in cell reinforcements present a lower PC

frequency.8-11 Asian populaces that have moved to the USA present a higher frequency of PC contrasted and those who stay in their nation of beginning. This is potential because of the reception of new dietary patterns dissimilar to those in their nation of beginning. This example upholds the thought that specific wholesome elements might adjust PC rates.

8 Smoking. Smoking has been related to expanded PC risk because of the expanded degrees of coursing cadmium increment cell oxidation. In any case, no causality has been laid out between these two circumstances.

9. Work out. Practice is viewed as a defensive variable, fundamentally for personal satisfaction regardless of PC, and subsequently is strongly suggested.

DIAGNOSIS

In the ongoing PSA time, a PC determination is made 5 to 10 years before side effects show up. As a rule, patients are asymptomatic or show side effects of urinary voiding as well as stockpiling connected with PC. These include diminished urinary stream, pushing, recurrence, desperation, and vesical tenesmus. High-level PC side effects incorporate bone agony, renal disappointment, hematuria, neurotic bone cracks, actual fatigue, and weight reduction. The most significant devices for PC findings are PSA levels (>4 ng/ml) furthermore, a dubious computerized rectal assessment (DRE) (e.g., expanded consistency or knobs). In any case, other factors can likewise build PSA levels without even a trace of PC: discharge, injury (e.g., rectal, transurethral catheter situation), aggravation, and contamination (intense prostatitis), as well as prostatic hyperplasia. There can be huge individual variety; in this manner, no less than two estimations required somewhere around 3 weeks separated are required.

One of the restrictions of PSA screening is that its high responsiveness and low explicitness lead to misleading up-sides. In certain nations, the reference esteem is set at 2.5 ng/ml, which has brought about numerous superfluous prostate biopsies (BxP) (80% of cases) and overtreatment. It is additionally worth focusing on that up to 5% of PCs don't show expanded PSA levels, so DRE might be the just viable symptomatic instrument. Up to 18% of PC cases are analyzed by DRE. Other PSA-determined estimations have moreover been portrayed, for example, PSA thickness, change zone PSA thickness, and other atomic strategies. In any case, these Public service announcement inferred estimations present restricted viable utility. Free PSA (<25%) is another valuable estimation at the point when the PSA level reaches somewhere in the range of 4 and 10 ng/ml, especially in patients who as of now have a negative BxP. In principle, a small part of this antigen can be delivered by hyperplastic cells, not by dangerous cells. In another test, the PCA3 marker from the non-coding prostate-specific mRNA is estimated in pee dregs that are acquired after prostatic back rub. The principal benefits of this technique over PSA are its higher responsiveness and explicitness and the way that it isn't connected with prostate volume or prostatitis. Nonetheless, its clinical utility is restricted, and its utilization is shown for patients with a negative BxP and an ever-evolving expansion in PSA.

CONTEXT TWO

FUN WAYS TO AVOID PROSTATE CANCER

Exercising should be a Habit

The advantages of activity are unfathomable number. Luckily, lessening your gamble of prostate cancer is on the rundown. On the off chance that you haven't been truly dynamic for some time, it's smart to gradually get once more into it. Swimming, strolling, running, and cycling is extraordinary choices. Try not to avoid getting others included all things considered. Bunch exercises can assist with adhering to practice objectives.

Practice is important for a sound way of life for everybody. For prostate disease survivors, practice however much you are genuinely capable, at a speed that is maximal for your wellness.

A few examinations have shown that fiery activity essentially decreased the gamble of prostate disease repeat, contrasted and a similar volume of activity at a simple speed. For those that can practice overwhelmingly, stroll as energetically as possible (3+ miles each hour), and attempt to add episodes of running. Enthusiastic activity ought to incorporate near maximal exertion, in which your heart beats quickly and you are perspiring. Such action incorporates running quick swimming or quick bicycling.

If you're not prepared for enthusiastic activity, sit back and relax. PCF-supported analyst June Chan, Sc.D. of UCSF takes note that patients can consider "Any smidgen of strolling, rather than sitting. Development is great for your general bone wellbeing. Try not to drive yourself to injury; simply get in a beneficial routine."

Research recommends that exercise influences energy digestion, irritation, oxidative pressure, invulnerability, and androgen flagging pathways. Past vigorous activity and strength preparation can be particularly useful in men on androgen hardship treatment (ADT) for cutting-edge prostate cancer, who are at a higher gamble of loss of bulk, osteoporosis, and of weight gain, metabolic disorder, and diabetes.

If you're new to working out, in therapy, or have progressed prostate cancer, counsel your medical care group to get an activity program custom-made for you.

Research has shown that exercise is protected, conceivable, and supportive for some individuals with the disease even while going through treatment.

Customary activity decreases your gamble of creating medical issues like coronary illness, stroke, and particular sorts of disease.

Curiously, normal actual work might assist with forestalling a few prostate problems and work on prostate wellbeing.

Prostate cancer patients have a few advantages over normal activity. A few malignant growth survivors vouch for expanding active work as it is connected with a decline in illness movement and an expansion in long-haul endurance.

Concentrates on malignant growth research have shown that this is especially evident in patients with cutting-edge prostate disease and going through androgen hardship treatment. Practice mediation likewise further develops the future of men with the confined prostate disease by over 10 years.

Altogether, exercise can lessen glucose levels, lower insulin levels, and lower prostate disease risk. It can likewise lessen the results of normal prostate disease medicines, like androgen hardship treatment (ADT) which causes muscle misfortune, fat addition, and osteoporosis.

Probably the most well-known benefits are recorded beneath:

Lessen sleepiness

Standard activity can assist with diminishing sleepiness levels in patients. Tragically, weariness is broad in patients going through disease treatment.

In any case, standard activity constructs bulk and works on joint adaptability and general molding, which beats the treatment impacts.

Forestall blood clusters

Extended periods of stability can prompt blood clusters, which might be perilous in the high-level stages. Practicing guarantees appropriate bloodstream all around the body, and staying away from clots is useful.

Works on psychological well-being

The actual activity works from the psychological standpoint of the patient. Disease treatment can be depleting, and it is not difficult to slip into sadness and tension. Notwithstanding, exercise can assist with combatting these mental issues.

Lessen coronary illness risk

Standard activity diminishes the dangers of heart infections among prostate cancer patients and diminishes the possibilities of osteoporosis and other ongoing circumstances, like coronary illness and diabetes.

Different advantages include:
- Forestall muscle misfortune and develop muscle fortitude
- Work on your equilibrium to decrease fall wounds.
- Forestall weight gain and corpulence, are connected to expanded malignant growth risk.
- Further, develop rest.
- Decline how much time you want to remain in the emergency clinic.
- Diminish the gamble of different tumors.
- Work on personal satisfaction.

What practice precautionary measures would it be a good idea for me to take?
Continuously counsel your PCP or medical services supplier before you start any activity program.

The right data about prostate disease and exercise is crucial.

More direction is required on what sorts of actual work are appropriate for patients relying upon sickness states and therapies in prostate cancer. Consequently, medical services experts ought to suggest fitted exercises, for example, obstruction activities to suit their requirements.

Prostate cancer and its medicines can cause explicit aftereffects that might expect you to change your activity program.

For example, vigorous activity is incredible; be that as it may, cycling isn't suggested for men with prostate disease because drawn-out bicycling can cause the bike seat to pressure the perineal region between the scrotum and the rear end.

Basic precautionary measures to take
To ensure that your work-out routine is all around as protected and charming as could be expected, avoid potential risks:

- Warm up and chill off accurately.
- Drink a lot of liquids.
- Watch for indications of overheating migraine, unsteadiness, queasiness, swooning, spasms, or palpitations, particularly in a sweltering, damp climate.
- Continue practicing after you recuperate, not when you are sick; allow yourself to stir back up to your standard level.
- Allow wounds to recuperate. However, that doesn't mean you want to surrender work out. For instance, assuming you've hyper-extended your lower leg while running, have a go at swimming or different exercises that utilize your arms and keep you off your feet.
- Dress in free, happy with apparel that is fitting for the climate.

- Focus on your environmental elements. For instance, be wary on the off chance that you walk or run, consistently face the traffic, and convey a telephone.

Additionally, assuming you experience any of the secondary effects beneath, quit practicing and illuminate your PCP.

- Weariness. Actual sluggishness can make it harder to enthusiastically work out. Screen your energy levels and adjust your activities appropriately.
- Myelosuppression. This condition implies you will probably wound and drain. Subsequently, you ought to utilize alerts with practice machines and hardware.
- Neutropenia. Disease treatment can cause neutropenia, which can leave you defenseless against contaminations, so stay away from places that are packed and not cleaned consistently, similar to exercise centers.
- Deadness. Fringe neuropathy is a typical symptom of malignant growth treatment. It could make it trying to convey loads securely assuming that it influences your hand, so offset preparing with tubing or groups ought to be liked.
- Lymphedema.

Different circumstances: You ought to likewise be mindful and affirm with your PCP if you can practice while having:

- Osteoporosis.
- Bone metastases.
- Cardiopulmonary issues.

Practice guide for patients going through prostate cancer treatment

The practice works on broad wellbeing. Various exercises are great for a protected and viable activity program during and after malignant growth treatment.

Exercising programs ought to incorporate avoiding PC.

High-impact workout

This fortifies your heart and lungs. Strolling is a simple method for getting oxygen-consuming activity.

The regular proposal for grown-ups is to get no less than 150 minutes of moderate activity. Then again, 75 minutes of overwhelming power movement every week is additionally adequate.

Moderate-power action has been displayed to further develop disease-related side effects. Be that as it may, it additionally gives upgraded alleviation from the results of radiation treatment, including outrageous sluggishness, rest issues, and mental issues like tension, wretchedness, and rest.

Also, oxygen-consuming activities, for example, cardiorespiratory wellness help to work on cardiovascular molding while at the same time keeping the body's creation.

Breathing activities.

Breathing activities further develop windedness or trouble relaxing. It likewise lessens any pressure and nervousness.

Extending

Extending further develops adaptability and stance, expands blood and oxygen stream to the muscles, and assists your body with fixing itself and its actual capability.

Balance works out

Loss of equilibrium can be a result of disease and its treatment. Be that as it may, balance activities can assist you with recapturing the capability and versatility you want to securely get back to your day-to-day exercises, forestalling wounds, like falls.

Strength preparing

Muscle misfortune frequently happens when an individual is less dynamic during malignant growth treatment and recuperation. It can likewise assist with battling osteoporosis, debilitating the bones that some malignant growth medicines can cause.

Strength preparing will assist with expanding bulk and bone thickness while diminishing muscle versus fat. It very well may be performed with loads, groups, machines, or utilizing one's body weight. Such activity will likewise forestall sarcopenia, which changes your fat-to-muscle proportion.

Kegel Activities

The muscle encompassing the prostate debilitates from malignant growth medicines like a medical procedure. One of the outcomes can be urinary incontinence, a deficiency of bladder control, and sexual brokenness.

Sexual brokenness can happen in prostate cancer because of diminished sexual longing and hormonal treatment that blocks testosterone. Likewise, nerve injury through medical procedures might build the recurrence of erectile brokenness.

Kegel activities can fortify your pelvic floor muscles. Regularly, these muscles support the bladder and entrail and capability to stop pee stream.

DIET CONTROL IS PARAMOUNT

What you eat can help or damage with regards to prostate disease risk. An eating regimen that is high in new natural products, vegetables, entire grains, and sound fats has been demonstrated to be valuable while dairy items ought to stay away. Food varieties that are high in lycopene are likewise perfect for bringing down the gamble of prostate disease so eat a lot of tomatoes and watermelons. At last, isoflavones have been displayed to have a comparative advantage and can be tracked down in tofu, peanuts, chickpeas, as well as lentils.

Research recommends that diet might assist with forestalling prostate cancer. Be that as it may, what impacts do the food sources you eat have on individuals previously living with the prostate disease?

Prostate disease is the second most normal malignant growth in American men, as per the American Malignant growth. Roughly 1 of every 8 men will get this finding during their lifetime.

What you eat may influence your viewpoint on this serious illness. Proactive dietary changes, especially if you eat a commonplace "Western" diet, may assist with working on your standpoint.

The effect of diet on prostate disease is effectively being investigated. The clinical Source referenced before proposes that a nutritious eating routine high in plant food varieties like products of the soil might assist with lessening the gamble of prostate disease.

An eating routine high in specific food varieties, such as handled meats and food varieties high in immersed fat, can affect wellbeing in various ways that might build the gamble for prostate cancer. This incorporates inciting oxidative pressure and aggravation and disturbing prostate chemical guideline.

Plant-based food sources, like vegetables, organic products, and vegetables, could make the contrary difference. Eating these sorts of food sources might assist in easing back the development of prostate cancer in the people who have it.

A Source observed that the Mediterranean eating routine, which is wealthy in vegetables, fish, entire grains, and vegetables, was related to a lower chance of prostate disease movement. A Source found that the Mediterranean helped generally speaking endurance rates after a prostate disease determination.

Food varieties to eat and keep away from

Plant-based and Mediterranean eating regimen approaches can assist with advancing wellbeing and further develop results in those with prostate disease. On the off chance that you might want to imitate these eating routine rules all alone, food varieties to eat include:

- Tomatoes and tomato items. Tomatoes are high in lycopene, a cell reinforcement that might defensively affect prostate wellbeing.
- Cruciferous vegetables. Vegetables in this gathering incorporate broccoli, bok choy, Brussel sprouts, horseradish, cauliflower, kale, and turnips. These vegetables are high in isothiocyanates, which might help safeguard against malignant growth.
- Vegetables and organic products high in carotenoids. Carotenoids are a group of cell reinforcements tracked down in orange and dull green vegetables, for example, carrots, yams, melons, winter squash, and dim green, verdant vegetables.
- Entire grains. High fiber, entire grain food varieties incorporate cereal, quinoa, grain, millet, buckwheat, and earthy colored rice.
- Beans or vegetables. Beans and vegetables are high in protein and low in fat. They incorporate soybeans and soybean items, lentils, peanuts, chickpeas, and carob.

- Fish. The Mediterranean eating regimen suggests fish as well as vegetables and vegetables.

It's what you eat, however, what you don't eat that considers well. For instance, scaling back handled and red meats super handled food varieties, and food sources and refreshments high in added sugar is critical to a decent eating routine.

The American dietary arrangement likewise suggests that you limit sugar-improved drinks as well as other profoundly handled food varieties and refined grain items.

Eating a more plant-driven diet might be smart for those with prostate disease, as certain examinations that diet high in specific creature items, including eggs and red meat, with additional serious types of prostate cancer.

SELF-MEDICATION

Supplements are normally an effective method for guaranteeing that you're getting every one of the supplements you want however they're not made equivalent.

A few investigations have shown that men who take Vitamin E alone will generally have a higher gamble of prostate cancer. Assuming that you take 1mg of folic corrosive, you may likewise be in danger. Calcium might have a comparative impact yet on a lot more limited size. To be protected, converse with your PCP before adding any enhancements to your daily schedule.

Research has proven that the growth in men results from taking supplements not prescribed by a medical practitioner. So, the need to stop self-medication is very important, as it is advised when you face certain medical challenges, and using the medical centers to adopt professional help is better. The result of taking supplements is a huge risk of having prostate cancer.

SMOKING

If you smoke cigarettes, you are bound to pass on prostate disease.

Stand by, how is this possible? The lungs are up there in the battle zone, breathing in all that smoke. The prostate is simply staying out of other people's affairs! How is it that it could be impacted by smoking a cigarette?

Indeed, it is, and in additional ways, than anyone would be aware, "Men who smoke, regardless of whether they have a conclusion of prostate disease, are bound to pass on from prostate cancer later on,". "Men who have been treated for prostate cancer who continue to smoke are bound to pass on from it, as well, since the disease is bound to repeat."

Smoking influences each cell in the body, and "cigarettes, when consumed, are viewed as complete carcinogens,"(cancer-causing specialists). See what occurs in the lungs of the drawn-out smoker: "Smoking causes DNA changes alongside irritation, and in emphysema and bronchitis, it fundamentally replaces the ordinary cells that line the lungs with scar tissue." Over the long haul, the lung harm from smoking resembles the development of sediment in the smokestack that can cause a fire. And the prostate? Does smoking reason irritation there, as well? The specific instruments aren't completely seen at this point, yet researchers are gaining ground. "For quite a long time, everyone thought smoking didn't have anything to do with the prostate disease by any stretch of the imagination," says Platz. "Goodness, were we off-base!"

Deadly and non-deadly prostate cancer are two altogether different things. Smoking doesn't appear to raise the gamble of second-rate prostate disease - the sort that is truly treatable, and as a matter of fact, may not at any point be dealt with. Yet, it raises your gamble of having malignant growth progress after finding, and it raises your gamble of kicking the bucket from the awful sort of prostate disease. "Smoking is outright terrible,".

Presently tell the truth: On the off chance that you're a smoker, did you simply coat over when you read that last sentence? "Smoking is awful - for what reason didn't anyone tell me?" said no smoker, of all time. Assuming that you're tired of hearing it, you're in good company. "Individuals have become weary of the smoking message,". "Yet, they have not heard it in that frame of mind of prostate disease."

DRINKING OF COFFEE

It's been said that every three cups of espresso can decrease your gamble of prostate cancer by as much as 11%. You need to gauge the advantages of the additional caffeine against the medical problems that are related to it. If all else fails, converse with your PCP.

Espresso is wealthy in dynamic fixings, cell reinforcements, and mixtures that can assist with forestalling cell harm and decrease aggravation. Concerning prostate disease, researchers have distinguished two malignant growth battling components that can dial back cell development: kahweol acetic acid derivation and cafestol.

Kahweol acetic acid derivation is a diterpene (a sort of hydrocarbon) that has mitigating properties and antiangiogenic bioactive mixtures. In a drug setting, antiangiogenic drugs are utilized to keep cancers from developing their veins, which can assist with easing back the development of malignant growth. Cafestol is a compound found in espresso that has comparable mitigating and antiangiogenic compounds as kahweol acetic acid derivation.

The measures of these two fixings are most elevated in unfiltered espresso beverages like a French press, as channels trap kahweol acetic acid derivation and cafestol. Curiously, it doesn't make any difference assuming you drink juiced or decaffeinated espresso - the aftereffects of lessening your gamble of prostate disease are something very similar.

The association between higher espresso utilization and prostate disease

A logical examination of past investigations uncovers positive discoveries connecting higher espresso utilization to a decreased gamble of prostate cancer. The information sees 16 examinations, 57,732 prostate cancer cases, and more than 1 million absolute review individuals. Contrasted with men who consumed zero to under two cups of espresso every day, the review saw as a:

- 1% abatement in the gamble of prostate disease with each extra mug of espresso.
- 9% decreased chance of prostate cancer in men who consumed two to nine cups of espresso every day.

- 7% diminishing in restricted prostate disease in men who consumed two to nine cups of espresso every day.
- 12% reduction in cutting-edge prostate disease in men who consumed two to nine cups of espresso every day.
- 16% reduction in lethal prostate cancer in men who consumed two to nine cups of espresso every day.

The concentrate likewise upholds proof that men who are now determined to have prostate cancer have an essentially decreased chance of sickness movement and repeat.

HEALTHY WEIGHT

Being overweight is one more issue that is normally connected with an expanded gamble of prostate cancer. While eating strongly and practicing ought to be sufficient to keep up with your optimal weight, that is not generally the situation.

While being overweight or large doesn't appear to cause prostate disease, it might build your gamble of fostering a forceful, quickly developing type of prostate cancer that is more challenging to make due. By shedding pounds, you might have the option to bring down your gamble of issues with prostate cancer.

The Connection Between Prostate Disease and Your Weight

Specialists don't know why, yet there is by all accounts a connection between your weight and prostate cancer.

The research proposes that being hefty may bring down your gamble of getting slow-developing malignant growth. Yet, it expands your gamble of getting a more forceful, deadly disease.

On the off chance that you're stout or put on a ton of weight after some time, your gamble of kicking the bucket from prostate cancer might be higher. You may likewise be bound to have prostate disease return whenever you've had it.

Why Weight Matters

Specialists don't completely grasp the connection between weight and prostate cancer. It could be connected with elevated degrees of cholesterol, estrogen, irritation, or metabolic changes that happen when you put on weight. Specialists need to concentrate on the issue more to grasp the connection.

Specialists are attempting to figure out additional distinctions in the metabolic cycles in large individuals, and non-fat endlessly individuals who've started eating less. They're attempting to perceive what weight means for cancer development and assuming growths get more modest when you shed pounds.

A few specialists figure sugar might assume a part. At the point when you eat sugar, your insulin spikes. Insulin is a known cell development factor for prostate disease.

It Is Great for You to Shed pounds
There's no demonstrated method for forestalling prostate cancer. Yet, working out, a sound eating regimen, and a solid weight might work on your general well-being and lower your opportunity of issues.

A few examinations highlight following a solid eating regimen that is low in fat and wealthy in products of the soil as a method for bringing down your disease risk. At the point when you work out, you lower irritation, help your resistance framework, and avoid medical issues. That may likewise bring down your gamble of malignant growth.

The most effective method to Shed pounds and Lower Your Gamble

Assuming you're conveying additional weight, you can lose it by cutting calories and practicing more. On the off chance that you're a sound weight, you can remain solid by eating great and practicing as a general rule.

To get more fit and lower your prostate disease risk, attempt these tips.

Keep away from sugar. A few specialists suggest avoiding straightforward sugars. Staying away from insulin spikes brought about by sugar might assist you with getting in shape.

Take a stab at scaling back food varieties that have stowed away sugars, similar to pasta, white bread, and white rice. At the point when you nibble, go after a modest bunch of nuts, a natural product, or vegetables rather than a sweet treat or sweet bite.

Follow a low-fat eating regimen. Scaling back greasy food varieties like meats, milk, and cheddar might assist you with getting in shape and lower your gamble of issues.

At the point when you cook, try not to add additional fat. Select lean cuts of meat. Pick low-fat or diminished fat dairy items rather than full-fat choices.

Eat more leafy foods. While it hasn't been demonstrated that particular supplements forestall prostate cancer, an eating regimen plentiful in products of the soil gives you nutrients and supplements that might decrease your gamble.

Products of the soil are additionally a decent substitute for less quality food sources like high-fat dairy or meats.

Filling your plate with a greater amount of them might assist you with shedding pounds.

Work out. Being dynamic is great for your general well-being. A few examinations likewise connect practice with lower prostate disease risk. Take a stab at practicing for 30 minutes generally speaking.

MASTURBATING

a few examinations directed over the most recent couple of years have for sure recommended that masturbation safeguards against prostate cancer. In reality, it was discharged, accomplished by one or the other sex or masturbation, that showed benefit.

Exactly how does discharge safeguard against prostate disease? One hypothesis is that it permits the prostate to get itself free from cancer-causing agents. All in all, masturbation may in a real sense clean your lines.

If you're no less than 45 years of age, you might have heard some abnormal childhood legends intended to deter you from jerking off. Messages about going visually impaired, losing your hair or developing hair on your knuckles, getting zits, and so forth may unexpectedly have expanded your interest. Presently, research recommends that more regular discharge - including masturbation - may safeguard grown-up men against prostate disease (PCA).

Bringing down prostate cancer risk

While medication isn't yet ready to change PCa risk factors, for example, hereditary qualities, impressive examination goes into the way of life changes that can bring down the chances of creating PCa. These incorporate things like eating routine, working out, stress the executives, stopping smoking, and keeping away from openness to ecological poisons. Now is the right time to put sexual conduct on that rundown.

21 times each month

The data on recurrence of discharge comes from concentration on polls given to more than 30,000 wellbeing experts who partake in the long-term Wellbeing Experts Follow-up Study. The survey doesn't ask how discharge was accomplished, so apparently, any demonstration prompting climax with discharge is incorporated, not simply intercourse. Isolating the information into age classes shows that as men age, they are inclined toward fewer discharges each month. The creators observed that the gamble of creating PCa was brought down by 20% for men who were discharged 21 times each month when contrasted with the individuals who were discharged 4-7 times each month. Strangely, "A comparative Australian review found the gamble was decreased by 36% when men discharged multiple times a week."

Nobody is precisely certain why recurrence can safeguard against PCa. A primary hypothesis has to do with the original liquid that is removed during the climax. It might free prostate tissue from specialists that cause disease, contamination, and irritation. To put it plainly, discharge helps keep the prostate sound.

Perspectives toward sexual conduct proceed to change, and discussing sex has become more open and less dishonorable. Therapists let us know that masturbation is a typical, sound piece of sexuality for all kinds of people. What's more, clinical analysts keep on instructing us on its relationship to by and large wellbeing. If to be sure, more incessant masturbation forestalls disease, it's uplifting news for prostates.

CONCLUSION

Prostate cancer is a gradually creating sickness. Early finding with the approach of public service announcement screening has been gainful, yet overtreatment is likewise a reality. The public service announcement test has high awareness yet low particularity. Until now, we can anticipate PC advancement in light of public service announcements, and research, yet we can't unequivocally foresee whether the PC will be lethargic or forceful. The patient's unquestionable requirement be involved all through the assessment no matter what public service announcement and DRE, as well as in the determination of the most reasonable treatment, going from perception to more extremist medicines. The best helpful arrangement will be the one that gives endurance the best nature of life and can be upheld by a multidisciplinary group.